Facebook Marketing:

30 Highly Effective Strategies for Business, Advertising, Generating Sales and Passive Income.

A.J. Robbins

Table of Contents

Introduction

I want to thank you and congratulate you for downloading the book Facebook Marketing: Facebook Advertising: 30 Highly Effective Strategies for business, advertising, generating sales and passive income.

This book contains proven steps and strategies on how to become an effective marketer on Facebook, one of today's most powerful advertising channels. Once you become familiar with the basics of Facebook advertising and follow the simple steps to get your account up and running, you'll be ready to tell the world about your product and watch you traffic and sales rise.

Here's an inescapable fact: 75% of today's businesses promote their products through Facebook advertising. Why? Because it works! But you don't have to be a Fortune 500 company or a Madison Avenue advertising heavyweight to experience success on Facebook, all you need to do is read this book.

If your business does not embrace the new media advertising opportunities available, odds are that your business will be left behind. More and more companies are moving away from traditional print and broadcast advertising and moving towards digital and social media.

This and subsequent generations of consumers are increasingly tech savvy and spend their lives with a mobile device nearby. They spend hours each day on social media channels, and Facebook is #1. As a business, you can't afford not to advertise with them.

And here's the good news: It's actually as affordable as it is effective! Learning how to establish a Facebook advertising account, to define and target your audience and how to create compelling content are just a few of the topics you'll learn while reading this book.

It's time for you to join the digital advertising age. Just follow this simple guide and you'll be on your way to reaching potentially millions of new customers where they spend their time online: on Facebook.

Chapter 1: More People Than China!

Think about this: Facebook has 1.49 billion members worldwide, and that number continues to grow daily. 1.49 BILLION ... That's more than the population of China. And with 22 billion ad clicks per year, Facebook has become the biggest advertising opportunity since search engines created a revenue model.

Your audience is on Facebook, and it's time for you to find them and to put your messaging in front of them. Facebook advertising is simple, it's affordable and anyone can run a successful campaign. But before we get into how to go about advertising on Facebook, let's take a look at some powerful numbers.

- Of Facebook's 1.49 billion users, 1.19 billion access Facebook from their mobile phone. They carry advertising potential with them in their pockets!

- The average user spends 40 minutes on Facebook each day.

- Facebook Advertising Revenue grew from $1.97B in 2010 to $12.47B in 2014. Advertisers understand the power of Facebook.

- Facebook accounts for more than 9% of all digital advertising, and 18% of global mobile advertising.

- 92% of social marketers are using Facebook for advertising.

- More than 30 million businesses now have a Facebook fan page.

The numbers don't lie. Advertisers are increasingly looking towards Facebook because of the incredible global consumer potential. And not just because of a built-in audience the size of China, but because the ads are targeted, cheap and effective.

Real People Vs. Keywords

Let's take a closer look at *why* Facebook Ads are more powerful than its biggest online advertising competition, which is search engine advertising such as Google AdWords, Yahoo or Bing.

With search engine advertising, advertisers are going after "demand fulfillment". They want a user who will actively search for something of interest based on keywords, be exposed to the ad they placed based on those keywords, and hope that the user will click the link and buy the product.

But there are limitations. For every product, there are only a few viable specific or related keywords that will work for advertising. And guess what? Your competitors are using the same sets of words. The search engines know this and will give higher priority to the advertiser willing to pay more for better placement. Before you know it, your CPC (cost per click) can more than double or triple.

In addition, you can only advertise your message to people who are actively searching for your keywords. Let's be clear ... search engine advertising has its place in your budget, but it should not be confused with Facebook advertising because the two are not the same and do not produce the same results.

With Facebook advertising, you are not relying on your audience searching for specific words or products. You are targeting who your customers are: their interests, hobbies, families, jobs, music, lifestyle, etc. You're targeting real people, not words.

An Example of Growth

Let's try this ... Imagine you're the owner of RVnGO.com and you're about to launch your new website marketplace for people who want to buy, sell and rent RVs in a peer-to-peer environment.

The website is functioning and your market is not only people who own RVs and want to monetize them, but anyone who likes the idea of maybe taking a vacation once in awhile. So basically, everyone.

With Google AdWords, you start bidding for keywords such as "RV Rentals," "RV Sales", "RV Vacations", etc. And yes, there are a TON of results and potential consumers interested in your product.

But here's the pitfall: Until your product came along, people have tended to search for RV rentals or sales through local and regional dealerships. They don't know that a larger peer-to-peer option even exists, so they search for a dealer in their area, or they go straight to Craigslist.

Your keywords are too generic and too localized for Google AdWords, and if you try to get more specific with the keywords you use, your target audience may not search for them. But you just KNOW that your audience is significant and you want to reach them.

So it's time to hit Facebook and reach your audience with more than just keywords: you'll hit them with images and lifestyle. Create an advertisement that speaks to the brand and lifestyle, not just the product. Target it to everyone in the United States ranging from 25 to 65 years old who like camping, road trips, tailgating, music festivals, sightseeing, etc. You're no longer waiting for someone to search your keywords, you're building an audience and generating demand among them.

In terms of conversion rates, you probably won't get the same percentage as with Google AdWords. But ask yourself this: would you rather convert 3% - 5% of the 200+ million Facebook users in the US, or 40% of the 150,000 or so people searching for RV rentals online?

Chapter 2: Setting Up Your Facebook Ads Account

Before we get into strategies, in this chapter you'll learn how how easy it is to set up your Facebook advertising account. You'll also learn all the important information you need to know about your account, including account permission management, spending limits, and other useful information that will help you to manage a smarter advertising campaign.

Even if you've already gotten your feet wet with an ad campaign on Facebook, you should still read this information and keep it handy. It's really important to understand how Facebook manages permissions between Pages, Apps, Events, and Advertising, as well as the limits your account is subject to.

This is paid advertising, so you will be asked for billing information before you can do anything. But it's an easy process and all you need is a valid credit card.

On the left hand side of the Facebook home screen, you should see a link for the Facebook Ads Manager. Click that and you'll be taken to the login screen. Log in with your information and you'll be taken to Account Settings. For a new account, give your account a simple name, such as the name of your business or Page.

Fill in all your personal and business information. Hit the "Save Changes" button and move to billing information (you can access it through the billing link on the left column of the ads manager).

If your primary card billing fails, all of your campaigns will be immediately paused until you pay the outstanding balance. You'll also have to manually restart them one by one. This is a tedious task if you're running several campaigns. If you have a secondary payment method set up, Facebook will begin billing your secondary method and everything will keep working smoothly.

To add your funding source, click "Payment Methods" on the left menu, right below "Billing". On the following page, you'll see that you have no funding source yet. Let's add one by clicking the "Add New Payment Method" on the top right of the page.

Unless you have a Facebook Ad Coupon, you have two options: Credit Card or PayPal. Once you reach high spending, you'll be able to agree to different payment terms with Facebook. For now, pick one of these two options and either insert the credit card data or authorize Facebook to bill your PayPal account.

You can access the Payment Methods page to edit your funding sources if you ever need to make a change. As you can see, there are links near each source that give you the option to make it your primary billing source or delete it. You cannot delete your primary source, so you'll need to make another option your primary source before removing your current primary payment method.

Facebook recently changed the way you get billed to make it more user friendly and less frequent. Your primary funding source will be billed every time you reach a certain billing threshold. The amount of this threshold varies based on your billing history.

This threshold will be pretty low when you first start advertising (usually $25), and you'll be billed every time you spend $25 in Facebook Ads. As you keep spending and your payments are correctly processed, your threshold will be automatically increased to $50, $250, $500, and finally, $750.

These thresholds don't have any direct impact on your advertising campaigns; they just affect how often you'll be charged. The big advantage of having a high threshold is that you'll have to deal with fewer invoices. If you want to change your threshold or have problems with billing, you can contact Facebook support.

Here you'll want to take note of the account spending limit. This limits the total amount of money that can be spent in Facebook ads for your account, and you can manage it from the billing page.

Setting the limit is very simple. Just click the "Manage" link and set it. Don't set it too low or you'll have to update it very often. Remember that each time the limit is reached, all of your accounts will be paused for at least 15 minutes.

As a final note, rest assured that the account spending limit doesn't have any impact on your ad delivery pace.

The Importance of Notifications

Advertising campaigns on Facebook require your utmost attention. First and foremost, as a beginner you'll want to monitor how your campaign is performing. It would be wise to check in on your campaigns daily up-to-date analytics, and change anything that may be underperforming. A great way to stay on top of your campaigns is to setup Notifications.

Facebook Notifications are a simple way to have Facebook send you updates right to your email inbox. However, you may experience an overwhelming number of emails if you don't setup which notifications you wish to receive, and how often. You can personalize all of this in the Account Settings page.

This is all pretty simple. Below your account information, you'll find two more blocks to manage your notifications: One for email and one for Facebook. Simply check or uncheck the boxes to be notified of each event.

Let's Roll!

Now that you've setup your Facebook Ads account, you need to decide what type of campaign you want to run. There are a number of different types of Facebook Ads and campaigns you can create and we'll discuss them in detail in the following chapter. Here's a snapshot of what you can do with Facebook Ads, depending on your goals and objectives:

- Boost your posts

- Promote your page

- Send people to your website

- Increase conversions on your website

- Get installs of your app

- Increase engagement in your app

- Reach people near your business

- Raise attendance at your event

- Get people to claim your offer

- Get video views

As you can see, Facebook has a wide variety of advertising and campaign options that can fit just about every need. You're just starting out, so remember to take some chances and try different campaigns. You'll be able to do this in a very affordable way, and you'll be able to see the analytics to tell you which campaigns are giving you the best ROI.

Chapter 3: What Are You Really Trying to Do?

The most important thing to keep in mind as you set out to advertise on Facebook is that not all campaigns are created equal. It's a common mistake among beginning Facebook advertisers to simply pump money into promoting your page and thinking that you're reaching critical mass. You may be building an audience, but does it fit in with the goals of your business? Are you simply getting page "likes"? Do they translate to actual conversions?

When you start advertising, you have to select an objective for your campaign.

The ads you place will automatically be optimized by Facebook to show to the people who are most likely to take actions that will help you achieve your objective. So for example, if you are advertising an app and your objective is to get more downloads, you probably don't want to spend money on Facebook's option to "raise attendance at your event".

More appropriately, you'll want to select "get installs of your app" so that your ads will be set up to show to the people within your target audience who are most likely to install your app.

Only you will ultimately know the the objective of your campaign, but Facebook does a pretty good job of guiding you through the process, and its categories are pretty intuitive. Let's look at them.

Boost your posts

When you choose "Boost your posts", you'll create an ad from a post you've already created on your business's Page. If your goal is to increase engagement on your post and get people seeing, liking, commenting on and sharing your Page content, then you might want to choose this objective. Here are some examples of what you can do:

Page Post Photo

This Facebook Ad type has the most space to show your beautiful pictures! Choose a compelling image that best suits your brand or lifestyle, and you'll be flooded with comments and Likes. You could also insert a link to your website in the text description of the post, but don't expect too much traffic from it.

Page Post Text

This ad format is focused on page engagement. However, there is very little reason to spend money here over the budgeting for more Page Post Photo ads ... images are simply more compelling than just text.

Promote your Page

When you choose "Promote your Page", your ad will be optimized to reach people in your audience who are likely to take the action of liking your Page. When people like your Page, your posts may appear in their News Feed, along with posts from their friends and family. Promoting your Page might be a good option if you want to engage with your audience or reach new customers.

Due to recent updates, a simple status update post on your page will only reach an average of 2-6% of your fan base organically. Promoting your posts is a great way to be sure that all your fans see your message.

Page Like

If generating more Page Likes is your goal for building your social profile, this is the Facebook Ad for you. The Page Like ad will be seen by your targeted audience and it will have a very specific action for users to Like your Page. When advertising for Likes, remember that it's not about getting the cheapest Likes, it's about picking the right audience that's interested in your page.

Send people to your website

One of the most common purposes of Facebook Advertising is driving traffic to your website. When you choose "Send people to your website", you can set a custom destination URL. For instance, you could send people to your website's homepage, online store, contact page or any page you want people to see. By default, your ad will be optimized to reach people who are likely to click on your ad.

The following is a look at the specific ways you can use Facebook Ads to drive people to your website:

Domain Ad

Of the different types of Facebook Ads, this one is the easiest to create. It can only be displayed on the right column, so there's no mobile support. You can choose a title, a short description, and the URL to be displayed. The number of characters are limited, so it pays to be very creative in just a few words. Domain Ads usually underperforms in terms of click-through rates (CTR), but these ads are very affordable.

Page Post Link

This is the most common of all the Facebook Ads, as it is ideal for promoting your external website. Page Post Link ads are Newsfeed Ads that feature a large image to catch user attention. The image should minimize overlaying copy, as you would be better served adding compelling copy to the post text and the link description. These ads typically perform well, and they have the added benefit of generating Likes for your page. Be sure to reply to all comments so that you increase your ad's engagement.

Multi-product

In June 2014 Facebook released a new Ad Format called Multi-product ad, which can be extremely useful for e-commerce advertisers looking to promote multiple products from their store.

Multi-product ads are similar to the Page Post Link ad, but they allow advertisers to add up to three different product links in one post. This is a significant benefit for e-commerce stores ... With just one advertisement, you can feature three different products each with its own image and unique link.

Increase conversions on your website

When you choose "Increase conversions on your website", you'll need to add a piece of code to the HTML on your website. You should add the code to a website page you want to track conversions on. For instance, if you want to track how many people saw your ad and then actually went and purchased the product you were advertising, you should add the code to the purchase confirmation page of your website. By default, your ad will be optimized to reach people in your audience who are likely to convert.

Get installs of your app

When you choose "Get installs of your app", you can create an ad with a link to the app store where people can install your app. If you want to measure the number of app installs, you can integrate your app with the Facebook SDK.

Mobile App

This is the perfect choice to drive more installs to your mobile app. This ad is displayed only on user's mobile newsfeed. When users click the "Install" call to action, the App Store will immediately pop up. This delivers a great conversion rate.

When using this Facebook ad format, you'll have many additional targeting options to fine-tune your audience. For example, you'll be able to choose which iOS/Android version you want the user to have, if you only want to target mobile devices or also tablets, and if you want to target only users connected to a Wi-Fi network.

Desktop App

This ad unit is relatively new and allows you to drive users to your Facebook app. Since Facebook apps are not supported on mobile, you can only target either the desktop Newsfeed or the right column.

Your app's rating and usage is well visible below the picture in your ad, so be sure to have at least a good score or you may lose the effectiveness of the ad. Would you play a game with a one-star rating.

Increase engagement in your app

When you choose "Increase engagement in your app", you can send people to specific areas in your app that you want people to go to. For example, you might send people to your online store. If you want to measure the success of your ad, you can integrate your app with the Facebook SDK.

Reach people near your business

When you choose "Reach people near your business", you'll target people in and around your local community by setting a radius around your business. Local Awareness may be the right choice for you if you want to increase in-store sales or foot traffic. Running a local awareness ad may also help you build awareness of your business in your local community.

Raise attendance at your event

When you choose "Raise attendance at your event", you'll create an event ad to get more people to see and respond to your event. People will get reminders and updates about your event, and you'll be able to see how many people responded interested and going.

Get people to claim your offer

When you choose "Get people to claim your offer", you'll create an ad with a coupon, discount or another special deal you want to provide. You can choose an audience for the ad you run and can decide how many people can claim your offer.

Get video views

When you choose "Get video views", you'll be able to create an ad that includes an embedded video. Video ads can help you tell a story as well as help build your brand on Facebook.

Video Advertising is still pretty new on Facebook, so it's very likely to drive high engagement. The downside is that producing a good quality video is very time consuming and expensive. Big brands are most likely to utilize this ad type because of their larger budgets, but video technology is making it easier for small companies with a smart social strategy to create quality videos with significant results.

So now that you know more about the different ad and campaign types available through Facebook Advertising, let's look at some examples of effective strategies in the next chapters.

Chapter 4: Every Picture Tells A Story

Once you've setup your ad's goal, it's time to design! The first thing to choose, and also the most important, is the set of images that you use.

Images are a powerful tool you can utilize for creating engaging, eye popping Facebook Ads. You don't need to be a world-class graphic designer to create compelling images ... but it does help if you know a little bit about tools such as Photoshop.

If you're at all unsure about your design or layout skills, it might be wise to hire someone who does know what they're doing. Don't worry, this doesn't have to break your bank. These days, there are a wealth of resources to find freelancers willing to create social media images for as little as $10. You probably even know someone who can create these pictures for you as a favor, but you don't want to have to go to that well too often.

Here are some tips for creating visually compelling Facebook Ads.

1. **Go crazy with the images!** As we've already discussed, Posts and Facebook Ads with images get much higher engagement than those without, as they help your ad or post stand out from a flooded news feed.

2. **Add multiple images to your ads.** Add multiple images to a Facebook Ad for extra variety and to test how different images coupled with your ad text perform. You can upload up to six images to accompany your ads at no extra cost, and these will automatically rotate every time a user visits or refreshes a page.

3. **For image ads, keep text under 20%.** Facebook advertising rules dictate that image-based Facebook Ads that are set to appear in users' news feeds won't get approved if the text takes up more than 20% of the image space. Facebook has a grid tool to help ensure that your image ad follows the guidelines.

4. **What size image should you use?** Facebook recommends uploading an image that is 1200x627 pixels for your ads. You'll be provided with more specific image size recommendations depending on the type of ad you're creating, but make sure your image is at least 600 pixels wide for appearing in the News Feed.

5. **Don't skimp on resolution.** There's nothing worse than seeing an online ad created by someone who obviously had no idea what they were doing. Blurry and pixelated images are amateur, and they are a real turnoff to consumers. Set the resolution of the images you are designing at 300dpi. You can save them in web-friendly formats such as .gif or .png to save on file size, but don't start small and expect a good looking finished product.

6. **Use Shutterstock.** Thanks to a recently announced partnership between Facebook and Shutterstock, you can access millions of stock pictures for free! It's very important to frequently refresh the images of your ads so users keep seeing them as fresh and attractive. Being able to immediately find and use new pictures for free is very useful (and will save you a lot of money).

Chapter 5: Words Tell Stories Too!

Writing your ad copy can sometimes be trickier than it sounds. Depending on your ad type, you will need to be very selective with the words you choose. For example, for Domain Ads or Page Post Links, you are limited to three short lines of copy: The headline, the text, and your News Feed link description (for News Feed ads).

•For headlines, you'll have up to 25 characters

•For ad text, you'll have up to 90 characters

•For News Feed link descriptions, you'll have up to 90 characters

For Page Like or boosted Post campaigns you have much more flexibility because you are writing copy for a full post. But you don't want to get too carried way ... while there are many types of Facebook advertising, the main idea is to get a user to click a link to somewhere else. You don't need to sell, you need to drive interest and response. Here are some tips to get users to do just that:

1. **Customize your ad headline.** When promoting a Facebook page, the automatic setup is for the ad headline to be the same as your page's title. Instead of leaving it as-is, type out your own customized ad headline to make the ad more enticing. Aside from your social media image selection, the headline is one of

the main ways your ad will make an impact (or fail to).

2. **Include a clear and direct call to action.** Include a call to action in the body text of your Facebook Ad to encourage Facebook users to take your desired action.

3. **Keep it short.** Concise posts tend to fare better than their lengthier counterparts – it's recommended that you trim down your words to somewhere between 100 and 250 characters for optimal engagement. No one's looking to read the next great American novel in their News Feed.

4. **Deliver shout outs with Facebook tagging**: Include tags in your posts. This is a great way to broaden your exposure, especially when working with other organizations. Back to RVnGO.com ... If you run a vacation destination and are running a promotion, tag them with an @RVnGO. When they see the tag, they'll be more likely to share your post with their fans, multiplying your reach by a ton! There's no reason not to be generous with tags. Tag conferences you're attending, businesses whose articles you're sharing, favorite clients, etc. Everyone likes to get noticed, and they'll remember that you were the one to put them in the limelight.

5. **#Hash it out:** As with tags, Facebook has enabled hashtags so you should use them. Twitter hashtags are a great tool for promoting a specific campaign you want to raise awareness for. It's a nice way to seamlessly connect Twitter and Facebook marketing

efforts. Hashtags also help categorize your posts by topic, and while the popularity of Facebook hashtags isn't exactly skyrocketing, you can search hashtag terms to discover fan conversations you may want to participate in.

We can't stress enough that whatever you do with your copy, keep it short and extremely clear. Facebook is not all about selling. It's about convincing users to click on the ad to discover more. Try to be catchy and clearly explain to users why they should click. Offering discounts and freebies usually helps. However, be careful not to attract too many cheap clicks that won't convert.

Chapter 6: The Right Place at the Right Time ... For the Right People!

With regard to ad placement, you have three choices when it comes where your Facebook Ads will appear: News Feed, Mobile, and right column.

Many marketers assume right column ads are a waste of money since they don't perform as well as News Feed ads. However, right side ads are relatively cheap and you'll never know which ad type is best for your campaign without testing. Give them a try.

Another thing to keep in mind is mobile targeting. Some advertisers make the mistake of sending users who click mobile ads to non-mobile optimized sites. Only use mobile advertising if your site is mobile-friendly otherwise you'll waste lots of money since Facebook mobile generates lots of clicks.

Removing a target is pretty simple. When creating an ad, you'll have three tabs to check a preview of it in the three available placements. At the end of each placement's tab you have a "Remove" link. Just click it to disable a placement.

Who Are Your Customers?

Getting to know who your customers really are is a crucial step for a successful Facebook Ads campaign. With more than 1.4 billion users with a Facebook account, it's absolutely critical for the success of your campaign to target only those who are potentially interested in your product.

Fortunately, Facebook offers a wide range of targeting options that will help you find the right audience! Facebook advertising is about getting customers, not cheap clicks. Choose the audience who'll see your ads and keep testing different targeting options to find the right mix. Here are some examples:

Demographic targeting

The first set of options to refine your audience is pretty straight forward: Basic demographic information such as the examples below. You know the market you want to reach, so just follow Facebook's instructions and you'll be able to easily define the audience that will see your ad.

> **Location**: From country to zip code, both big brands and local shops can target their potential customers.

> **Age**: Do you want to appeal to teenagers, young families, or retired people? You have the flexibility to choose any age range.

Gender: Target specific genders. Now that Facebook offers over 50 gender options, this is much more useful for some businesses than other ad platforms.

Facebook recently improved these options giving you much more granularity over who will see your ads. Clicking on the "More Demographics" button will offer you a wide range of options for every need.

Just click one of the targeting topics in the menu and you'll be able to refine your audience based on many options. As an example, you'll be able to target people by their political views, life events, job titles, ethnicity, and so on.

When using these advanced options, always keep in mind that some of them only apply to United States citizens and may not work outside of the country. Finally, since they're pretty new, they often return a very small target audience. Be careful not to limit too much your reach.

Interest Targeting

Interests are one of the best Facebook ads targeting options as they allow you to target people specifically interested in a subject related to your product. For example, you could target people interested in your competitors or your broader market segment, or magazines and blogs covering your market.

> **Precise Interests**: Precise Interest Targeting lets you target your audience based on their profile information. This includes their likes and interests, apps they use, Pages they've Liked, and more (you can even target your competitors' fans!). Start typing an interest and a list of options will appear. You can also click "browse" to see some broad categories suggested by Facebook. Once you've added some interests, Facebook will also recommend similar ones. Adding more than one interest will target people with at least one of them so you'll make your reach broader.

> **Behaviors**: Unlike Precise Interests, behaviors allow you to target people by purchase history, intent, and more. This data is gathered by Facebook analyzing many factors and also using external data sets. They are not always useful, but when they are they work great! As an example, you can target people currently traveling or planning their next trip ... priceless if you're in the

hotel or event booking market. Check them out and see if they can work for your business.

Connections

The Connections option can be very powerful for your Facebook ad targeting, especially if your business has a strong Facebook following already. It allows you to target people who are fans, friends of fans, or not fans of your Page, app, or event.

Here are some ways you can use advanced connection targeting for your ads:

1. **Get new Page Likes**: Exclude your current fans and targeting only new potential fans

2. **Improve reach:** Increase the reach of your Facebook posts by targeting your fans and their friends. The likelihood that these people will re-share your sponsored content goes up significantly.

3. **Target your fans' friends**: Provide social proof for consumer products by targeting your fans' friends. This works much better for B2C than niche B2B products. Targeting your industrial engineering products at a mechanical engineer's friends probably won't generate much business.

Custom Audiences

There's a reason why Facebook has decided to insert this once-unknown feature as the first targeting field in their new ad's creation interface: Custom Audiences are an extremely powerful way to target users.

Here's how it works: If you have a list of email addresses, phone numbers, or Facebook user IDs of people you know are interested in your product, you can upload this list to Facebook. This list will be used to create a Custom Audience containing all the people Facebook found using your list.

This is very exciting because it's basically the missing link between the Facebook world and all your external data. The possibility are endless. You can target your existing customers to upsell new products, newsletter subscribers to convert them into customers, and so on.

Fully explaining how to create Custom Audiences and all the endless opportunities linked to them is outside the scope of this guide. However, if you're serious about Facebook Advertising, you must start using them now.

Once you have your Custom Audiences created, just start typing the names of people on your list in this field and they'll show up. You can target multiple Custom Audiences and even exclude them from your ad targeting. For example, if you're running a campaign to get more users to sign up for your product, you may exclude a list of all those that already did.

Chapter 7: More Tips & Tricks

This last chapter is just a list of some great additional ideas to keep on mind when planning your Facebook Ads campaign.

1. **Go in with established goals.** Do you want more website visits? More Facebook likes? More fan engagement? Each of these metrics has its own value, so choose your main objective before you get started. The Facebook ad type you go with will depend on what you're trying to achieve. Facebook's new advertising scheme guides you to recommend ad formats based on your primary goal.

2. **New to Facebook advertising and not sure where to start?** Try starting with the Page Likes objective – you'll build your audience and encourage folks to like your page. More likes make you look popular, which encourages more people to like you in a domino effect – it's a safer alternative to buying followers on social media.

3. **Try Facebook Offers to capture attention!** Facebook Offers works similar to the Google Offers Extensions, letting you promote a deal exclusively to Facebook users. Try using an offer to give away an item – maybe an eBook or whitepaper – in exchange for an email address. Or create an offer or discount to be redeemed in your brick and mortar store. It's recommended that you target your first Facebook Offer to just your fans. If it

goes over well, then you can widen your net to larger audiences.

4. **Use your Facebook ads to highlight special deals.** Facebook paid advertising can be used to call attention to your latest deals and sale events.

5. **You don't need a Facebook Page to create a Facebook ad.** You can create an ad for a website by selecting the Clicks to Website objective or the Website Conversions objective. Be aware though that Facebook ads not connected with a Facebook page will appear exclusively in the right column, not in the News Feed.

6. **Try activating Sponsored Stories as an add-on.** When someone interacts with your Facebook page, offer, event, etc. the action triggers Facebook posts, or "stories," that the user's friends may then see in their News Feed. These "stories" are generated naturally but are often buried in the News Feed. Opting for sponsored stories basically means you are paying to increase the likelihood that these stories will be seen. You can opt in or out of sponsored stories in the left column of the ad creator tool.

7. **FB ads can do more than you think.** Using Facebook for advertising can help you promote a page, app, or even an event! Exercise all your options.

8. **Let others help with your ads.** When you add another administrator to your Facebook ads account, they can stop and edit

promotions for your page. To add another admin, go to Ad Manager > Settings > Scroll down to Ad Account Roles > Add a User. The user must either be your friend on Facebook or have their email address be searchable on Facebook. Simply choose their access level and click Add.

9. **Selecting a bidding option.** You can choose from a number of different bid setups for controlling Facebook advertising costs. You can bid for clicks, impressions, or your desired objective (e.g., Facebook page likes). If you choose the recommended (and selected by default) option of bidding based on your objective, your bid will automatically be set to help you reach your objective, whereas bidding for clicks or impressions allows for more customization.

10. **Choose between daily or lifetime budget.** As an advertiser, you can choose to set up a daily budget or a lifetime budget. A daily budget controls how much you will spend on a specific campaign per day. Your ads and sponsored stories stop showing once you hit your daily ad budget, helping your budget Facebook advertising rates based on each daily cycle. Lifetime budget lets you select how much you want to spend over the entire span of time a campaign is scheduled to run. Don't forget that each campaign has a separate budget, so create a social media marketing plan to keep Facebook advertising prices within your comfort zone.

11. **Want to change your ad campaign?** You can edit your campaign's end date or budget anytime after the campaign has started running. While you can't change your minimum daily spend limit (it's set at $50), you can change your daily ad budget, which ultimately is what really controls the cost of Facebook advertising.

12. **Keep an eye on your potential audience meter.** As you add targeting options and narrow your audience, Facebook will generate an approximate number of people you'll reach. This is only an estimate, but can help you make sure you're not targeting too many people (or too few). Ads perform best when they're targeted to at least a few thousand people, so consider removing some restrictions if your audience is dipping below this.

13. **Want to bring customers in store?** Try targeting people who live in your town or local area. Couple this with Facebook Offers to be redeemed in store and see just how much in-store footfall you can get from being social.

14. **Host a Contest!** In the past marketers were required to use a third-party application for FB contests, but Facebook recently changed their policy and now allows contests to be hosted directly on Facebook. Hosting a giveaway or contest on Facebook has never been easier!

15. **Hide valuable content behind a Like barrier.** Hiding valuable content behind a like barrier will get more likes to your page – be

sure to include a colorful and captivating call to action graphic to seal the deal.

16. **Try a large photo instead of the auto-generated article box.** Trying to drive traffic to a blog post or article you're sharing? Instead of using the automatically generated link and image block generated by Facebook, attach your own larger social media pic to the post and add the link to the blog post as a neat and tidy bitly URL. A larger image can do a better job of capturing attention. A/B test this technique and see if your clicks improve from the regular auto-generated format.

- **Option #1:** Text with auto-generated link box with small image.

- **Option #2:** Insert text with a bitly link to the article and upload a separate image.

- **Option #3**: Add text with bitly URL. Create custom image with text overlay and upload it to attach to your post. This is a bit more work but can really pay off.

17. **Update your cover photo.** Change your Facebook cover to mix things up. Changing a cover photo to reflect a season or time of year shows fans that you are making an effort to be active and stay relevant. Updating your cover photo to advertise a special sale or giveaway will also help those events get more attention than they might receive otherwise.

18. **Post frequently and consistently.** Don't worry about overdoing the posts – as

long as they are spaced evenly through the day, you'll be fine. Only 16% of your fans will see one post (if even that), as news feeds easily become over populated. The more you post, the better your chances are of being seen. However, do remember to focus on quality over quantity – every post should be of value, not just something thrown quickly together.

19. **Use Facebook Insights to measure your success.** Insights lets you see your most popular and successful posts in terms of link clicks, shares, and likes. This data is extremely valuable and ignoring it is like ignoring conversion tracking for AdWords – it's just plan silly! You should be using this data to see what you're doing right, and then do more of it.

20. **Share testimonials on Facebook.** Testimonials are always powerful, and that rule continues on Facebook. However, it's good to think outside the box when delivering testimonials on a social network. Rather than bland words, incorporate photos, videos, or other media.

21. **Ask questions!** Facebook users love to get their voices out and feel heard. Try incorporating questions or surveys into your posts for engagement. Keep the questions simple though – no one feels like filling out the SATs on Facebook.

22. **Participate in fun themed posts:** Joining in on weekly movements like #ThrowbackThursday or posting about goofy holidays gives you a chance to have fun with fans.

23. **Share exclusive content for Facebook fans.** Posting special, top secret content just for fans on Facebook adds a sense of exclusivity and belonging for your following. Post information or tidbits they might not find elsewhere.

24. **Share fan-created content.** Sharing fan-made content is a great way to bolster a true sense of community among your followers. It shows that you care and makes fans feel valued and appreciated – who doesn't want that?

25. **Fill in the blanks.** Another strategic post format to drive engagement is the fill in the _____ tactic. Users' eyes are drawn to the _____, and getting eyeballs is half the battle. Make sure to incorporate a large colorful photo for added attention. Track your engagement metrics and see how the post performs!

26. **Photo captions.** Asking for users to provide a caption to an exciting or laugh-worthy photo is another smart strategy to drive interaction and engagement.

27. **Don't quote me on this, but quotes rock.** Posts involving inspiring or life-affirming quotes often perform very well. For an added bonus, attach a photo to your quote – even better, do Pinterest-style image/quote overlay. People eat that stuff up!

28. **Jump on the meme wagon:** Memes work on the same principle as quotes, but with auto meme generators they are easier to create.

Folks love 'em though! We create our own PPC memes from time to time and they tend to do well.

29. **Have users "vote" with the Like and Share buttons.** As we've said, people love to express their thoughts and opinions on Facebook. Sometimes they like it too much, but you might as well have those soapbox speakers benefit you! Ask users to choose option A or option B, with a vote for A as a "Like" and a vote for B as a "Share." You'll get some of both and will broaden your post reach and engagement a TON. The more controversial the topic, the more engagement you'll be likely to see.

30. **Let us know in the comments.** You can always get your audience to comment if you invite them to do so. Not only does this help boost your Facebook engagement, but it also helps with SEO!

Conclusion

Thank you again for downloading this book!

I hope this book was able to help you better understand the basics of Facebook advertising and how you can maximize the potential to promote your business.

The next step is for you to test out a few of the tips and tricks to find the ones you like most and that are the best fit for what you are hoping to accomplish. Set your campaign and watch the traffic roll in!

Finally, if you enjoyed this book, please take the time to share your thoughts and post a review on Amazon. It'd be greatly appreciated!

Thank you and good luck!

A.J. Robbins

www.ingramcontent.com/pod-product-compliance
Lightning Source LLC
Chambersburg PA
CBHW070419190526
45169CB00003B/1324